The Atlantic Alphabet Beach Song

Phyllis Levine

Loconeal Select

The Atlantic Alphabet Beach Song

Copyright © 2009 Phyllis Levine.

Illustrated by J. Newman

All rights reserved. No part of this publication may be copied, reproduced, stored, archived or transmitted in any form or by any means without prior written permission from the author. Published in the United States by Loconeal Select, an imprint of Loconeal Publishing, LLC.

www.loconeal.com

First edition, Wasteland Press: January, 2009
Second edition, Loconeal Select edition: June, 2013

ISBN 978-0-9885289-7-0 (Paperback)

*To Deanna and Lauren,
and to all who have affection for
the carefree times spent by the sea.*

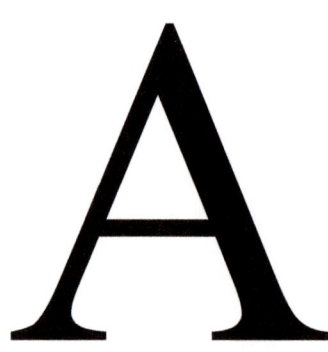

A Is the Atlantic that woos me come in.
Agile and Anxious I run and I spin.

B Is the Bather who wears a Big grin,
Bravely and Briskly decides to jump in.

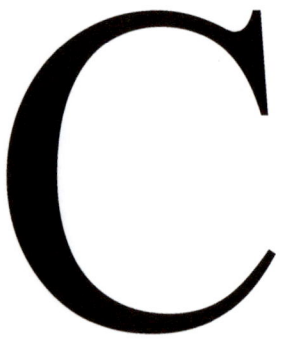

C Is the Crab that tries to Catch toes.

D Is the Deep Diver splashing my nose.

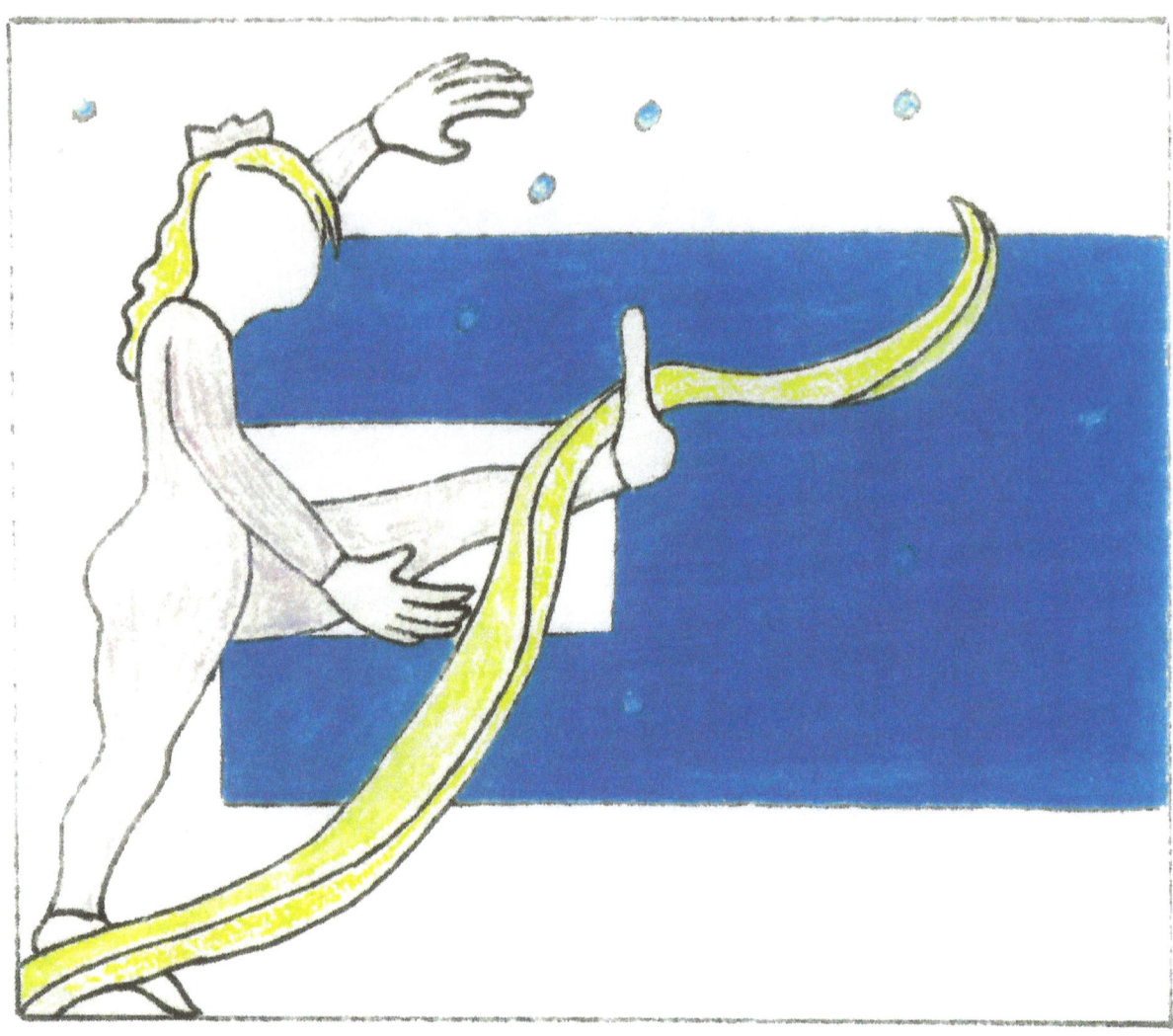

E   Is the Eel Easing over my feet.

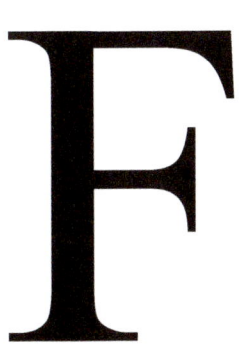

F Is the Fast Fish, that simply won't speak.

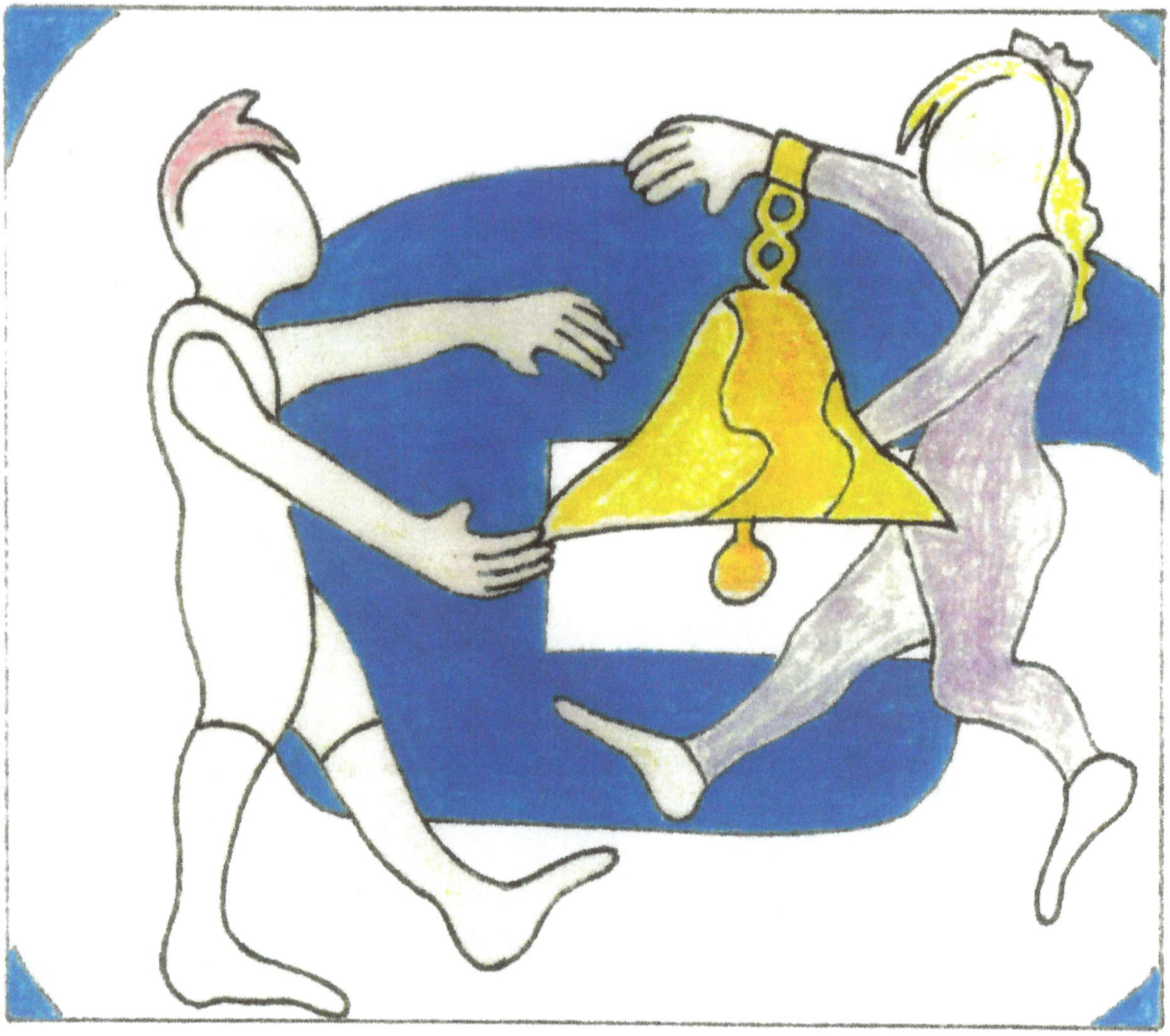

G Is the Gong of the mighty ship's bell,
that Glitters in Glory, along the canal.

H Is the Happy Hat pulled over my ears,
so the sun will not burn me,
and make me grow tears.

I Is the Indigo color of shells,
and for Ice-cream that sticks
on my sandals and towels.

J   Is the Jogger that passes in haste.

K Is the Kingfisher who glides to my pace, ignoring the Kite that flew off to space.

L   Is the Long Lighthouse toot-tooting its horn.

M   Is the Moon just Missing its call.

 Is the New Night that tip-toes to sea,
then Nudges the owl to hoot back to me.

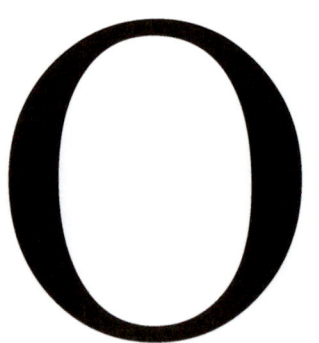

O Is the Ocean that swirls about me,
painting the sky a red Orange
only for me.

P Is the Pelican alone on the Pier.
It Peers out at the fisherman,
and then disappears.

Is the Quizzical Quilt of the sea who hides nymphs inside bubbles, for me not to see.

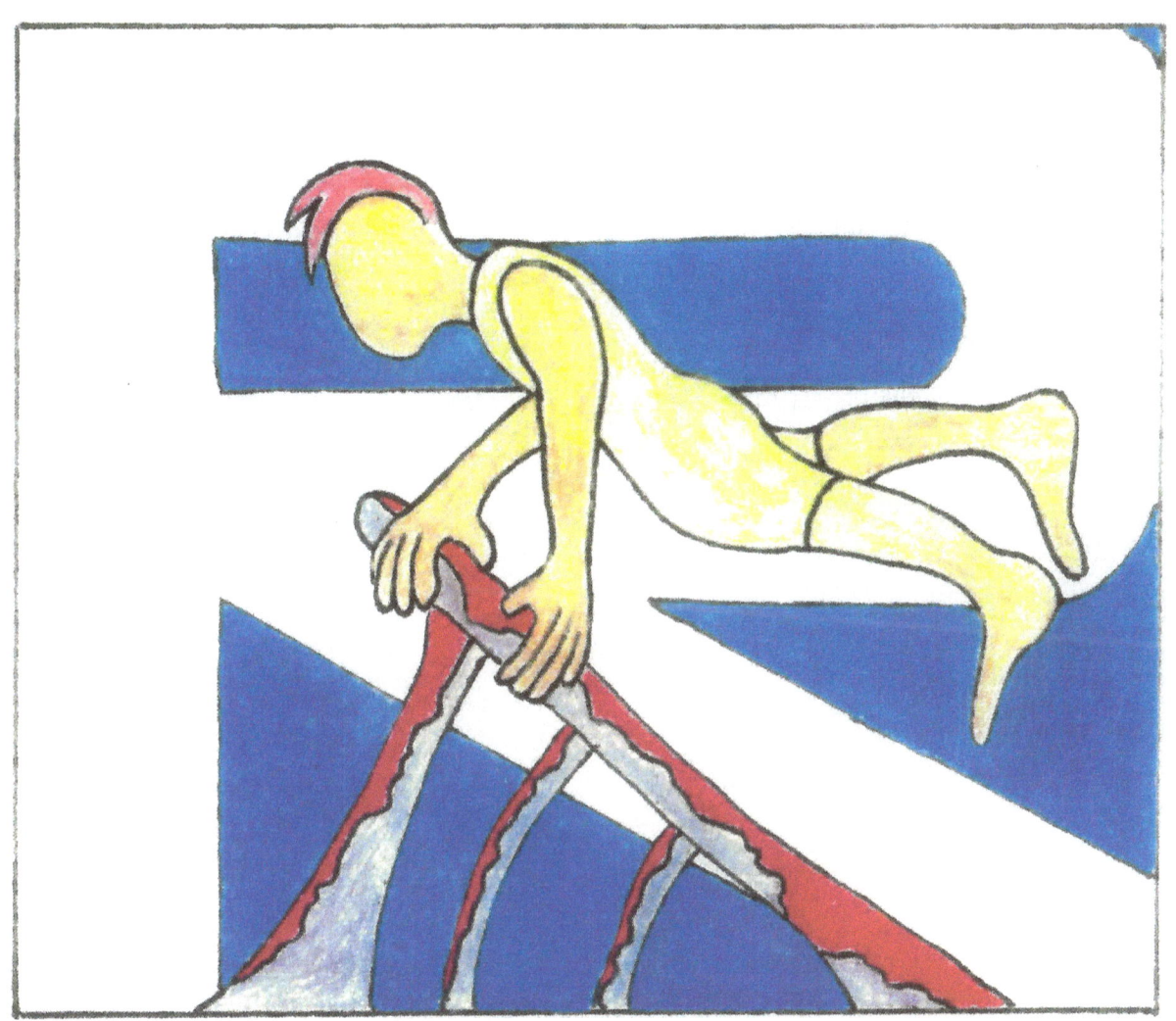

R Is the Rider who upsets the Right sail, clinging ever so tightly to the Rusty old Rail.

S Is the Seagull, Sandpiper and pail, and Soft Sand that keeps footprints but Simply won't tell.

T Is the Tall Tent,
built from Tiny Tee shirts.

U	Is the Umbrella to hide me from spurts, that covers me Up and Unties me from hurts.

V Is the Vendor
who sells mustard and pickles.

W Is the Wide Wave that Whispers and giggles.

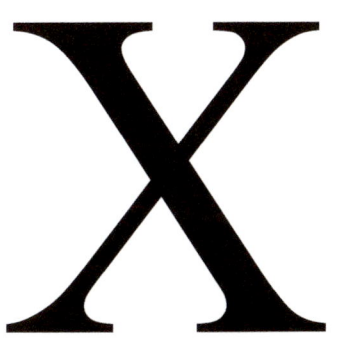

X   Is the Xebec that drifts on the sea.
It sings of its travels,
and salutes back to me.

Y Is the Yacht to sail me on course.
It gathers me Yonder,
to seek a sea-horse.

Z Is the Zephyr, the breeze from the sea.
He Zips through sand-castles that wash out to sea,
and softly tells Zelda to imagine with me.

www.ingramcontent.com/pod-product-compliance
Lightning Source LLC
Chambersburg PA
CBHW041540040426
42446CB00002B/175